D0535940

Rural Homes

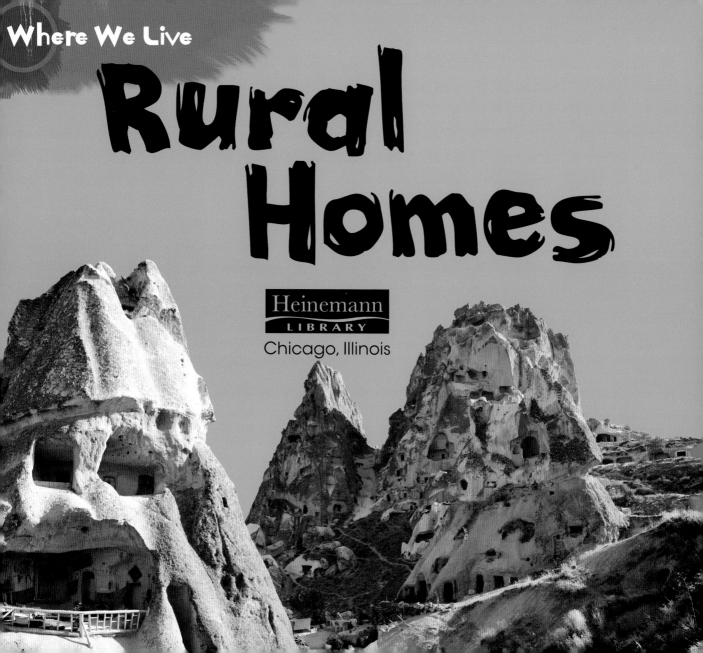

Heinemann
LIBRARY

Chicago, Illinois

Edited by Daniel Nunn and Abby Colich
Designed by Cynthia Akiyoshi
Picture research by Mica Brancic
Production by Sophia Argyris
Originated by Capstone Global Library
Printed and bound in China at RR Donnelly Asia Printing
Solutions

ISBN 978-1-4329-8066-5 (hc)
978-1-4329-8071-9 (pb)
17 16 15 14 13
10 9 8 7 6 5 4 3 2 1

Library of Congress Cataloging-in-Publication Data
Smith, Sian.
    Rural homes / Sian Smith.—1st Edition.
        pages cm.—(Where we live)
    Includes bibliographical references and index.
    ISBN 978-1-4329-8066-5 (hbk.)—ISBN 978-1-4329-8071-9
(pbk.) 1. Housing, Rural. I. Title.
    HD7289.A3S65 2013
    307.72—dc23   2012046423

Acknowledgments
We would like to thank the following for permission to
reproduce photographs: Getty Images pp. 4 (National
Geographic/Joy Tessman); 6, 23 bottom (Flickr/Ulrike Maier);
7, 23 centre bottom (AWL Images/Peter Adams); 9 (Robert
Harding World Imagery/Eurasia); 12, 23 top (AFP Photo/
Sabah Arar); 14 (AFP Photo/Rizwan Tabassum); 15 (Lonely
Planet Images/Aldo Pavan); 16, 22 bottom right (Oxford
Scientific/Trevor Worden); 18, 22 bottom left (Robert Harding
World Imagery/Dallas & John Heaton); 19 (Photographer's
Choice RF/Cristian Baitg); 20, 22 top right (Digital Vision/
John Clutterbuck); 21, 23 centre top (Lonely Planet Images/
Mark Daffey); Shutterstock pp. 5 (© Rob Marmion); 8 (©
Radu Razvan); 10 (© S Reynolds); 11 (© Chrislofoto); 13,
22 top left (© iPics); SuperStock p. 17 (hemi/Hemis.fr/Franck
Guiziou).

Front cover photograph of huts of the Tairona Indians,
Colombia, reproduced with permission of Shutterstock
(© urosr). Back cover photograph of a log cabin in Lapland,
Finland reproduced with permission of Shutterstock (© iPics).

Every effort has been made to contact copyright holders
of material reproduced in this book. Any omissions will be
rectified in subsequent printings if notice is given to the
publisher.

Contents

Why Do People Need Homes? . . . 4

What Does Rural Mean? 6

Rural Homes. 8

What Are Rural Homes Made Of? 12

Unusual Rural Homes 16

Neighbors 20

Around the World 22

Picture Glossary. 23

Index 24

Why Do People Need Homes?

People live in homes.

Homes keep people safe.

What Does Rural Mean?

village

When something is rural, it is in the countryside. Villages are in rural places.

Rural places are far away from cities and large towns.

Rural Homes

There is more space to keep animals and grow plants in rural places.

farmhouse

Some people live on farms.

Some people live on ranches.

Some rural homes are large and have big yards.

What Are Rural Homes Made Of?

reeds

People sometimes use the materials around them to build rural homes.

log cabin

Many homes are made of wood.

Some homes are made of mud
or clay.

Some homes are made of stone
or brick.

Unusual Rural Homes

stilts

Some homes are on stilts.

Some homes float on water.

Some homes are under the ground.

Some homes are in caves.

Neighbors

Some people in rural homes live far away from their neighbors.

Some people in rural homes live close to their neighbors.

Around the World

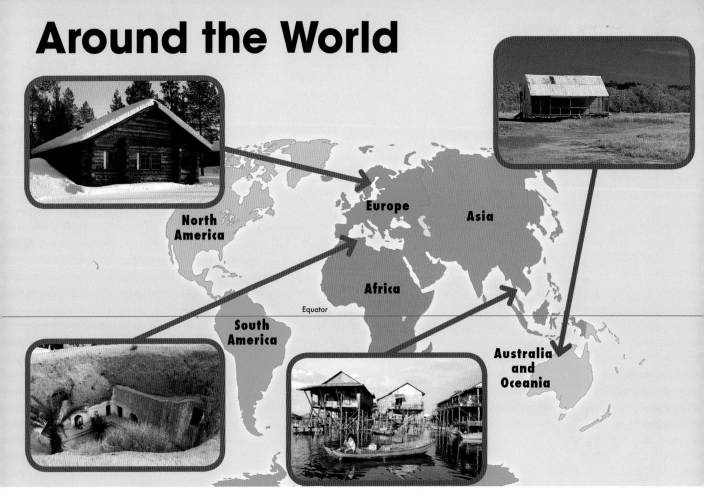

Follow the arrows to find out where each of these homes are found.

More information on page 24

Picture Glossary

material what something is made from. Wood and stone are types of material.

neighbors people who live near to you

rural countryside or places far away from cities

village place where people live in the counryside. A village is smaller than a town.

Index

countryside 6

caves 19

farms 9

neighbors 20, 21

ranches 10

stilts 16

villages 6

yards 11

Photograph information

The photographs in this book were taken from the following locations: p. 4 Namibia, Africa; p. 5 Viñales, Cuba; p. 6 Longsheng province, China; p. 7 Ethiopia, Africa; p. 8 the Alps, Switzerland; p. 9 Gwynedd, Wales; p. 11 England; p. 12 Najaf, Iraq; p. 13 Lapland, Finland; p. 14 Hyderabad, Pakistan; p. 15 Dang village, China; p. 16 floating village on Tonle Sap, Cambodia; p. 17 Chong Khneas floating village, Cambodia; p. 18 Matmata, Tunisia; p. 19 Uchisar Capadoccia, Turkey; p. 20 Broome, Australia; p. 21 Amantani Island, Peru.

Notes for parents and teachers

Introduce the children to the word *rural*. Explain that rural places are in the countryside where there's lots of space and fewer buildings (unlike cities and towns) and that there are rural places all over the world. Read the book together and ask the children what they think it might be like to live in the different types of rural homes. Discuss the materials the homes are made from and any special features. For example, homes made from mud or clay and homes that are under the ground tend to stay cool in hot weather. Look at the pictures on pages 20 and 21 together. Why do the children think it would be important to have good neighbors when you live in a rural place? Encourage the children to draw a picture of their favorite type of rural home and to write a sentence describing it.